From Songs to Smart Contracts:
An Introduction to Crypto

From Songs to Smart Contracts

An Introduction to Crypto

Sam Brooker

Nashville

Published 2026

ISBN 979-8-234-00790-2 (paperback)

Table of Contents

Foreword

This book exists because of my wife. Yes. It's true.

Before I understood blockchains, wallets, or smart contracts, there were conversations — usually late at night, usually starting with, *"Okay, check this out…"* I'd try to explain what I was learning and why it felt important. Half the time I assumed I was rambling and boring her.

She never made me feel that way.

She listened. And then she asked questions.
Not surface-level questions — *good* ones. The kind that make you pause and realize you don't actually understand something as well as you thought you did.

Those conversations became a sort of co-write. Not in code. Not on paper. But in thought. We'd bounce ideas back and forth, poke holes in them, reshape them, and slowly form a clearer picture of what this new world could look like — and why it mattered in the first place.

Her belief in me is never loud or flashy. It shows up quietly: in patience when I went down technical rabbit holes, in encouragement when things felt confusing, and in trust when I decided to stop watching from the sidelines and start building. She inspired me to learn deeper, not faster — and to ask better questions along the way.

So while my name is on the cover, this book carries her fingerprints all over it. It's dedicated to her — for believing in me, for sharpening my thinking, and for walking beside me as I learned how to grow into a new chapter….

But I'm still a song writer in my heart.

You can check out my new single (ERC20) on the blockchain ;)

Chapter 1: Introduction — The Virtual Stage

Picture this: It's 2007.

I'm in my Nashville apartment — t-shirt and baseball cap on, Mackie soundboard in front of me, guitar in hand. Across the room sits my buddy Jeremy Lister, one of the most talented singer-songwriters I know.

But tonight, we're not in some smoky bar on Broadway. We're playing in a nightclub I just built — inside a video game.

I'd bought virtual real estate in Second Life and built a digital club for live music. My avatar was dressed in a sharp black suit like I belonged at the Grammys. My real-life outfit? Let's just say it was more "late-night taco run" than red carpet.

We went live, and avatars from all over the world started showing up — dancing, clapping, cheering. For a moment, it felt like the future.

And maybe it was.

We didn't make any money that night — but afterward, we sat down at a virtual poker table and played for Linden Dollars, Second Life's in-game currency.

Then I discovered something that blew my mind: You could trade Linden Dollars for real U.S. dollars.

"Wait… I just made money in a video game that I can spend in real life?"

That was the spark. I didn't know it yet, but it planted the seed for everything that came next.

I've always been a creator.

I toured as a Warner Brothers artist, spent years playing music across the country, and eventually launched an independent music publishing company.

Our first big hit? "Cruise" by Florida Georgia Line — the longest-running #1 country song of all time.

Since then, I've had songs placed in films and TV shows — proof that something written in my living room could travel across the world and live on forever.

In a way, smart contracts are like that. Lines of code I write today can live forever on a blockchain, outlasting me and impacting people I'll never meet.

After taking a break from the music industry, my wife and I launched KOKOS, Nashville's first low allergen, plant-based ice cream shop — again, building something that didn't exist yet, something people needed.

Through every chapter of my life, I've avoided the beaten path. I've always been willing to try something new, take a risk, and create what no one else had done before.

Crypto was no different — except the ride was wilder, the stakes were higher, and the lessons came fast.

My First Crypto Rollercoaster

By 2018, Bitcoin was everywhere. Your uncle was talking about it at Thanksgiving. News anchors had suddenly become "crypto experts." It felt like a gold rush.

So I jumped in with $10,000.

I watched Bitcoin skyrocket to $19,000 and thought, "I am a genius. Early retirement, here I come."

Then… it crashed. Hard.

I traded my way down the rollercoaster, learned the painful lesson of market cycles, and by 2019, I'd built back up to 3.16 BTC — worth about $11,000 at the time.

But we had just opened KOKOS. Bills were piling up. I got nervous.

So I sold. Regretfully.

Today, those 3 coins would be worth close to $400,000.

Maybe I wouldn't be writing this book — or maybe I'd be writing it from a beach, drink in hand. Either way, that experience taught me something critical:

Markets move in cycles. Boom. Bust. Build. Repeat.

You either learn to respect the cycle… or you get chewed up by it.

Why This Book Exists

Since then, I've gone deeper — launching DeFi tokens, experimenting with tokenizing real-world assets, and starting the BlockFoundation.us , a nonprofit using blockchain technology for philanthropy.

Now I want to share everything I've learned — the wins, the mistakes, the moments of celebration, and the nights I stared at my screen thinking, "What did I just do?"

Because here's the truth: the world is changing — whether we understand it or not.

The real question is this:

Will we learn to ride the wave —

or let the old system keep drowning us?

This isn't a textbook. It's not a boring economics lecture.

This is a story. A conversation. A roadmap to help you stay free, stay informed, and play a real part in shaping what comes next.

By the end of this book, you won't just know what crypto is — you'll understand why it matters, how it works, and how to be part of it…

…without getting wrecked. (That's crypto slang for losing money. See? You're already learning)

Chapter 2: What Even Is Crypto?

Let's start with the question everyone's secretly afraid to ask out loud:

What even is crypto?

You've probably heard the buzzwords — blockchain, Bitcoin, Web3 — and thought, "That sounds complicated."

Good news: it's not magic. And you don't need to be a computer scientist to get it.

At its core, crypto is just money on the internet — with one very important twist:

It's money that doesn't need permission.

I've had countless late-night, spark-filled conversations with my wife about this topic. Sometimes I think I'm boring her — only to realize she *sees* it too. Our talks about crypto have become a kind of "co-write," like the songwriting sessions we used to have. We bounce ideas off each other, shaping a shared vision of what this new, unknown path might look like. In fact, she's the reason I'm writing this book — the reason I was able to dive deep and learn how to build...how to understand this seemingly complicated abstract thing....let's simplify it like we did.

It's money, But Upgraded

Before we talk about crypto money, let's talk about regular money.

Money has three basic jobs:

1. Store of Value — You can save it today and use it later.

2. Medium of Exchange — You can trade it for stuff.

3. Unit of Account — It gives prices meaning.

But here's the problem: governments keep printing more of it.

And the more money they print, the less yours is worth.

(Hello, $7 latte. I see you.)

Banks charge fees, set rules, and sometimes even block you from accessing your own funds.

Crypto was created as a way to solve that.

Crypto's Big Idea

Crypto moves money to the blockchain — a giant, public spreadsheet that everyone can see, but no one can secretly change.

Think of it like Google Docs for money:

- Every transaction is tracked.

- Everything updates in real-time.

- Everyone can view it — but no one can fudge the numbers behind the scenes.

Instead of a single bank updating your balance, a network of computers all around the world agree on who owns what.

- No middleman.

- No permission needed.

- No banker side-eying you for sending $1,000 at 2 a. m.

If traditional banking is a gated community with armed guards, crypto is an open road — anyone with a wallet can drive on it.

The First Coin: Bitcoin

The first use case for this tech was Bitcoin — a digital version of cash that's scarce. Only 21 million will ever exist.

That scarcity is what gives it value.

It's like digital gold.

And just like gold rushes of the past, Bitcoin attracted dreamers, skeptics, builders, and outlaws. That's part of what makes it so exciting.

My 2018 "Where Has This Been All My Life?" Moment

When I first learned about Bitcoin in 2018, I was stunned.

"How in the world did none of my friends ever mention this?!"

If I'd heard about it in 2011, I would've jumped in without blinking.

Even today, when I mention crypto, most people give me that look — half curious, half concerned about my mental well being and some with a sense of panic that they don't understand it themselves.

That's part of why I'm writing this book — to turn that look of what the heck are you talking about into a spark of curiosity.

Why You Should Care

Crypto isn't just a get-rich scheme or a tech fad.

It's a new financial system — one that's being built in real time.

And you can use it.

Here's what it unlocks:

- Send money globally in seconds, for pennies — no banks needed.
- Artists can sell directly to fans — no label taking 85%.
- Entrepreneurs can raise money globally, without begging a bank.
- Anyone with an internet connection can join the world economy.

This chapter is your "You Are Here" pin on the map.

From here, we're going to zoom in:

- How Bitcoin actually works.
- What Ethereum unlocked.
- How you can participate — safely.

Let's break it all down — one block at a time.

Chapter 3: The Bitcoin Origin Story

To understand where crypto is going, you have to know where it came from.

And like any good origin story, it starts with a problem.

The Spark: The 2008 Financial Crisis

It was 2008. Banks were collapsing. The housing market was imploding. People were losing homes, jobs, retirement accounts — their sense of stability.

Trust was shattered.

And in the middle of that chaos, a mysterious figure named Satoshi Nakamoto posted a nine-page PDF online: The Bitcoin Whitepaper.

It wasn't a rant. It wasn't a protest sign. It was a blueprint.

"What if money could work without banks?"

It proposed a brand-new kind of money — one that didn't require middlemen, bailouts, or permission.

And it hit a nerve.

The Mystery of Satoshi

Nobody knows who Satoshi is.

Some say it was one brilliant programmer.

Others believe it was a group — cypherpunks obsessed with privacy and freedom.

Then there are the theories:

- Was the timing — just after the global meltdown — too perfect?
- Was it a grassroots movement… or a quiet test by governments?

Was Bitcoin the answer to the crash… or part of the plan?

And the strangest, Satoshi Nakamoto translated from Japanese "Wisdom/ Intelligence of Central Origin).

We may never know. But one thing's clear:

Bitcoin showed up exactly when people were ready for something new.

It became a symbol — not just of digital money, but of personal sovereignty.

Blockchain: The Secret Ingredient

At the heart of Bitcoin was something revolutionary: blockchain technology.

Imagine a giant Google Doc that:

- Anyone can read
- No one can secretly edit
- Every change is timestamped, verified, and permanent

That's what Bitcoin introduced. A ledger of truth, maintained not by banks or governments, but by a network of independent computers around the world.

No trust required. Just math.

It was money that didn't ask for permission — and didn't need your bank's blessing.

Mining: The Digital Gold Rush

Bitcoin was also designed to be scarce.

There will only ever be 21 million BTC. That's it.

No printing more. No emergency supply injections.

Instead of a central bank, Bitcoin is "mined" — created by computers solving complex math puzzles. When a miner solves one, they earn some new Bitcoin.

It's like a digital version of panning for gold:

- But instead of a pickaxe, you need a graphics card.

- And instead of a riverbed, you're in a server farm.

Halvings: Built-In Scarcity

Here's where it gets brilliant — every four years, the mining reward gets cut in half. This is called a halving.

Imagine waking up and all the gold mines in the world are producing 50% less gold… overnight.

That's what Bitcoin does, by design.

Historically, each halving has been followed by a bull run — a euphoric surge in price — followed by a crash.

Then builders step in. Then it happens again.

Boom. Bust. Build. Repeat.

Why Bitcoin Still Matters

Today, Bitcoin is the most secure, decentralized, and battle-tested network of money ever created.

It's been declared dead by the media over 400 times.

It's survived exchange hacks, government bans, and endless waves of doubt.

And it's still here.

You don't have to be a hardcore Bitcoin believer to see what it represents:

- Money that no one can inflate at will

- Money that moves without middlemen or borders

- Money that belongs to you — and only you

Whether Bitcoin becomes global currency, a hedge like digital gold, or simply the spark that lit a revolution…

…it changed everything.

Chapter 4: Ethereum and the Smart Contract Revolution

For a long time, I was laser-focused on Bitcoin.

It was the king. The headline-grabber. The OG coin.

Ethereum? I didn't really get it.

I dabbled here and there, traded it now and then, but mostly thought of it as "that other coin."

Then I built my first smart contract.

And it clicked.

Ethereum wasn't trying to replace Bitcoin.

It was building a whole new dimension.

If Bitcoin was the first chapter in crypto's story, Ethereum was the sequel — and it changed everything.

What's a Smart Contract?

Let's slow down.

A smart contract isn't some legal document you sign to rent an apartment.

It's a tiny program that runs on a blockchain.

Think of it like this: "If X happens, then do Y."

Once it's deployed, no one — not even the person who wrote it — can alter the rules.

Imagine a vending machine:

- You insert money.

- The machine checks if it's enough.

- If yes, you get your snack.

- No cashier. No approval. No price switcheroo mid-transaction.

That's what Ethereum brought to the table: Trustless, automatic execution — in code, not contracts.

Ethereum = The Internet's App Store

Bitcoin is like a pocket calculator. It does one thing — and does it well: send money.

Ethereum is like a smartphone.

It runs apps.

Just like the App Store has games, banking, and social media, Ethereum has dapps (decentralized applications) for:

- Trading

- Lending

- Art

- Fundraising

- Gaming

- Voting

This turned crypto from a currency into an ecosystem.

What People Built on Ethereum

Let's make this real:

- Trading Apps: Like a farmer's market where anyone can set up a booth — and buyers trade freely. No middleman.

- Digital Collectibles (NFTs): Like rare baseball cards or original paintings — but digital, and provably yours.

- Online Clubs (DAOs): Group chats with shared bank accounts and a voter based built-in democracy.

- Banking Without Banks (DeFi): Loans, savings, and investing — no permission needed.

Ethereum made money programmable.

That single shift opened up everything.

Who Runs Ethereum — and Why It Matters

Ethereum was created by Vitalik Buterin, a teenage genius and crypto believer, along with a crew of builders.

They wanted to decentralize not just money, but the rules of interaction online.

But even Ethereum has its controversies:

- Some say it's still too dependent on a few big holders.

- Others criticize high fees and slow transaction times.

- Some think it's just the beginning — and something better will replace it.

You don't need to solve those debates now — just know Ethereum is powerful, imperfect, and evolving.

My First Time Deploying Code

The moment I deployed my first smart contract…

It felt like writing a hit song again.

But this time, I wasn't launching it into the radio ether — I was launching it into a global, permanent network. The Block Chain.

It was live. It was immutable. And it was mine.

And it was… a total mess.

The first smart contract I built from scratch? Total flop. I accidentally left the mint function open — meaning anyone, at any time, could create more tokens. Unlimited supply. Zero scarcity. Basically the blockchain version of printing monopoly money.

Who wants a token with unlimited supply and zero purpose?

Not me. Not anyone.

But that's how you learn.

By messing up on-chain, in public, and figuring it out as you go.

That first mistake made me a better builder. It made crypto feel real — not just numbers on a screen, but a tool you could break, fix, and reshape with code.

I went from crypto user to crypto participant. And I never looked back.

Why Ethereum Matters to You

Even if you never touch code, Ethereum affects you.

Most of what people now call Web3 — NFTs, decentralized art markets, crypto games, crowdfunding platforms — started on Ethereum.

It proved we could:

- Store value

- Make agreements

- Exchange assets

...all online, borderless, and automatic.

If Bitcoin gave us digital money...

Ethereum gave us digital rules.

Together, they created a digital world anyone can build in.

And that's where we're heading next — into the open town square of DeFi, where finance becomes permissionless, peer-to-peer, and maybe even fun.

Chapter 5: What Is DeFi (and Why Should You Care?)

Now that we've explored Bitcoin and Ethereum, let's take a stroll into our imaginary virtual "Crypto Town". I'll try to paint a picture of something relatable for this abstract concept.

Our Little Town is buzzing with life. In the center sits a glowing, oversized piggy bank — humming softly, coins clinking inside.

People wander by:

- Tossing tokens in
- Swapping them out
- Lending a little here
- Earning a little Interest there

And here's the magic: everyone's here for a different reason.

- Someone's buying their morning coffee.
- Someone's starting a business — halfway across the world.
- A teenager is snagging a ticket to a virtual concert.
- An artist is getting paid instantly for digital art.

It all happens in real-time. No gatekeepers. No permission needed.

Banking Without the Banker

Here, you are the banker.

You decide when to deposit, lend, trade, or earn.

No "banking hours." No minimum balances.

No guy in a suit asking why you're withdrawing your own money.

- Want to earn interest? Go for it.

- Want to swap tokens at 3 a. m.? Be my guest.

This is DeFi — decentralized finance.

It’s not a bank. It’s a protocol — code that runs 24/7, open to anyone, anywhere.

Liquidity Pools: The Town Piggy Bank

At the center of it all is that glowing piggy bank.

It’s called a liquidity pool — and it’s the beating heart of DeFi.

People fill it with pairs of tokens, and anyone can walk up, toss in one token, and take out the other.

There’s no teller. No cashier. Just automatic trades — governed by smart contracts.

When one side of the token pool runs low, the code quietly adjusts the exchange rate — to keep the balance flowing.

Every trade leaves behind a tiny thank-you fee, which gets split among the people who stocked the pool in the first place.

They’re not bankers.

They’re participants.

And they get rewarded.

Becoming a Liquidity Provider

When you add your pair of tokens to the pool, you get a receipt: an LP token (Liquidity Provider token). It proves your share.

Now you're earning a piece of every trade on that pair.

You've gone from user to infrastructure.

It's like your tokens took a side job while you sleep.

Yield Farming: The Town Garden

Want to earn even more?

Take your LP token and plant it in the garden.

This is yield farming — where protocols reward you for helping them grow liquidity.

The more helpful your tokens, the more fruit they bear.

Just don't forget where you planted them…um which wallet? (Been there.)

Staking: The Town Safe

Some protocols reward you for locking up your tokens — like putting them in a time-locked vault.

You can't touch them for a while, but they'll reward you for the commitment.

This is called staking — and it keeps networks secure while you earn passive rewards/tokens.

The Wild West Warning

But let's be honest: this is still a frontier town.

Sometimes, the code has a bug — and a token pool drains overnight.

Sometimes, a shady dev runs off with the funds. (Slang=Rug)

Sometimes, a token crashes so hard, you wake up to find half your portfolio vaporized before breakfast.

I've felt both extremes:

- Waking up a little richer than the night before

- And watching my balance drop like a rock

DeFi is powerful — but it demands respect.

The upside is real.

So is the risk.

My First Real Leap Into DeFi

DeFi was my first adventure away from Coinbase — away from the comforts of a huge company keeping watch over my holdings.

Until then, Coinbase had been my training wheels. Easy. Safe. Familiar. But I knew if I wanted to actually understand this space — to own it — I had to take full control. That's when I discovered DeFi. Decentralized finance. No middlemen. No customer support. Just me, a wallet, and the blockchain.

It was the first time I sent BTC off a centralized exchange and into a wallet I controlled.

There was no safety net.

No “undo” button.

If I messed this up... there was no one to rescue me — or my money.

It was exciting.

It was nerdy.

It was technical.

And I loved every second of it.

That was the moment I realized crypto wasn’t just something I held.

It was something I used. Something I commanded. Something I owned.

Why This Matters

For the first time in history, anyone — anywhere — can access financial tools that were once reserved for banks, brokers, or billionaires.

- A teacher

- A truck driver

- A teenager with a phone

Everyone gets a seat at the table.

Understanding DeFi doesn’t mean becoming a day trader.

It means knowing your options. Choosing for yourself.

Being part of the system — not just watching from the outside.

This is finance rebuilt from the ground up.

And it’s just getting started.

Chapter 6: What Is a Wallet?

The first time I created a crypto wallet, I felt like I was opening a secret vault.

Except no one gave me a key.

No one asked for ID.

No one said, “Welcome to the financial revolution, Sam.”

Instead, a string of strange words popped up on my screen — like a haiku written by a robot on mushrooms:

“glory… cactus… winter… muffin… liberty… shadow…”

This, I would learn, was my seed phrase.

And this… was the beginning of true ownership.

What Even Is a Wallet?

A crypto wallet doesn’t hold your crypto.

Let’s get that out of the way.

Your coins live on the blockchain — always.

Your wallet just holds the keys to access them.

It’s like:

- Your crypto is the house

- The blockchain is the neighborhood

- Your wallet is the keyring

Lose the keys, and you can’t get in.

Private Key vs Public Key (The Basics)

Every wallet has two keys:

- Public Key: Like your email address — you give this to people so they can send you crypto.

- Private Key: Like your email password — never share it, ever. It gives full control.

The private key is the only thing standing between you and your funds.

And the terrifying beauty of crypto is:

There’s no "Forgot My Password" button.

You either control the key — or you don’t.

The Seed Phrase: The Master Key

That random list of words?

It’s not a weird poem.

It’s your seed phrase — a human-readable version of your private key.

With this one phrase, anyone could rebuild your wallet from scratch — even on a different device.

Lose it, and your crypto is gone.

Write it down.

Store it offline.

Engrave it in titanium if you must.

But whatever you do, don't screenshot it.

Hot Wallets vs Cold Wallets

All wallets fall into two categories:

- Hot Wallets: Connected to the internet (like MetaMask, Trust Wallet). Convenient, but vulnerable.

- Cold Wallets: Offline (like Ledger or Trezor). Safer, but slower.

Here's how I think about it:

Hot wallet = your checking account.

Cold wallet = your fireproof safe.

You might carry some cash in your pocket, but you wouldn't store your life savings in a backpack at a music festival.

My Early Wallet Mistakes

I've:

- Sent tokens to the wrong address

- Lost access to a wallet by clearing my browser

- Misplaced my seed phrase during a move

- Thought I "lost everything" — twice — only to recover it an hour later

Every one of those moments aged me 3 years.

But each one also made me more sovereign.

More resilient.

More in the driver's seat.

Not Your Keys, Not Your Coins

You've probably heard this before:

"Not your keys, not your coins," says the controversial DeFi crypto "King" Richard Heart. And he's 100% correct.

But it's not just a meme saying.

It's the foundation of crypto.

If your crypto lives on a centralized exchange, it's not really yours.

It's an IOU.

It's the promise that the exchange probably has your funds and will probably let you withdraw them.

But in DeFi?

With your own wallet?

You hold the keys.

You are the vault.

That's what I felt the first time I moved funds from Coinbase into MetaMask.

It wasn't just a transaction.

It was a transformation.

I wasn't just watching crypto anymore.

I was in it.

Chapter 7: Not Your Keys, Not Your Coins — For Real This Time

Let me be blunt:

If your crypto is sitting on a centralized exchange… you don't really own it.

It's not yours. It's a balance on a spreadsheet. It's a claim on an asset — not the asset itself.

The Day My Favorite Exchange Froze Withdrawals

I won't name names. (Okay fine, it rhymed with "schloincase.")

One day, I logged in to check my balance — a nice little collection I'd been dollar-cost averaging into for months.

I hit Withdraw.

And I saw a spinning circle. Then a message:

"Withdrawals are temporarily disabled."

No timeline. No reason. No access to my funds.

And suddenly, I remembered the phrase I'd heard a thousand times in podcasts and Twitter threads:

"Not your keys. Not your coins."

It hit different this time.

What You Really Have on an Exchange

Here's what you actually "own" when your funds are on a centralized exchange:

- An account.

- A password.

- An interface that says you own crypto.

But behind the curtain? The exchange holds the real keys.

They decide who can withdraw, when, and how.

Sometimes they freeze withdrawals. Sometimes they get hacked. Sometimes they go bankrupt — and your funds go with them.

Remember Mt. Gox? FTX? BlockFi? That's not ancient history. That's last year.

Why People Ignore This

It's convenient. That's the real reason.

- You don't want to mess with wallets.

- You don't want to risk typos or hacks.

- You trust the platform to handle things.

I get it. I really do.

But convenience is a trap.

The more convenient it feels, the more risk is hidden behind the curtain.

Self-Custody Isn't Optional — It's Crypto's Core

Crypto was invented so you could own value directly.

No bank. No custodian. No permission.

That only works if you hold the keys.

The second someone else does, you're back in TradFi — just with shinier logos.

I Lost Access to My Wallet Once

Not my funds. Not a hack. Just... me being totally irresponsible.

I moved a small stack of tokens to a hot wallet I hadn't used in a while — totally forgot to export the seed phrase. New laptop. Gone.

That moment was terrifying… and oddly clarifying.

Because I realized something:

This is what owning crypto really means.

It's not just a number on an app. It's a responsibility. A practice. A discipline.

So What Should You Do?

- Use centralized exchanges to buy and sell. Sure.
- But don't park your savings there.
- Learn to use wallets — even if it's uncomfortable at first.
- Back up your seed phrase. Twice. Offline.
- Start small. Practice.
- Make self-custody a habit, not a someday plan.

Learn From My Mistakes

Be organized. Don't wing it. Don't trust yourself to "remember it later."

Don't:

- Write seed phrases on paper.
- Take pictures of them.
- Hide them in random folders on your laptop.

Do:

- Disconnect from Wi-Fi when generating a new wallet.
- Use a fireproof safe.
- Consider a safety deposit box.
- Etch your seed phrase into a metal plate — yes, really.

These phrases can last 100 lifetimes if you treat them right.

One day, when the world feels like actual Star Wars, some kid might find your steel seed relic...

... and become a crypto zillionaire in your name.

That's legacy. That's sovereignty. That's what self-custody makes possible.

This Isn't About Paranoia. It's About Empowerment.

Holding your own keys isn't about preparing for collapse.

It's about understanding the tools. Taking full ownership. Becoming a builder, not just a buyer.

This is the point where crypto becomes real.

Not flashy. Not speculative. Yours.

Chapter 8: The Rise of the Crypto Community — Vibes, Values & Velocity

Crypto isn't just code.

It's people.

It's Discord servers, DAOs, memes, mission statements, and late-night group chats full of strangers building together.

Crypto is a movement pretending to be a market. A philosophy disguised as an asset class.

It's the most collectively chaotic, radically optimistic, and deeply human thing I've ever been part of.

From Music Scenes to Meme Chains

Before crypto, I found community on stages.

I was surrounded by musicians and fans — all vibing to the same frequency. That moment when the room breathes as one? That's what I loved.

Then I walked into a Discord server and saw 200 people riffing on a token design… building out governance… memeing their own roadmap.

No one was in charge. Everyone had a role.

I thought, "This feels familiar. This feels like a band."

Only this band had a treasury, a roadmap, and a legal entity registered on-chain.

What Is a DAO, Really?

DAO stands for Decentralized Autonomous Organization.

Which sounds like a villain headquarters from a Marvel movie.

But really, a DAO is a group of people with a shared mission — and a shared wallet.

- No CEO.

- No HR department.

- No office cubicles.

Just smart contracts, community votes, and meme-powered momentum.

A DAO is like if a startup and a subreddit had a baby, and that baby could fund itself.

Wait... This Is Where My Kid Hangs Out?

I didn't find crypto community in some polished enterprise Slack channel.

I found it on Discord — the same app my son used to talk about video games and Roblox.

He used to laugh at me because I didn't even know how to make an account.

"Dad… it's not that hard."

I had to ask him how to join a server.

Even now? Discord still confuses me sometimes. Channels everywhere. Bots. Emojis I don't fully understand.

I'm a dad. A pretty cool one. But not that cool.

So I started hanging out on Telegram instead.

It felt more natural. More like texting. More like something a crypto-curious musician-dad could handle.

The Vibe Layer

Here's the part no whitepaper explains:

Vibe is infrastructure.

If you've ever walked into a Telegram group or Twitter Space and immediately felt something — you get it.

Some communities feel:

- Cultish

- Corporate

- Chill

- Chaotic

- Brainy

- Bro-y

- Beautiful

And you choose your own tribe, Or start your own tribe.

You don't need to be a coder or a trader. You can show up as:

- A writer

- A community lead

- A moderator

- A meme lord
- A vibesmith

In Web3, the whole stack matters — not just tech, but tone.

The Speed of Shared Belief

These communities move fast.

One day you're asking questions in a DAO's onboarding chat…

Three days later you're helping launch a proposal that moves $50,000 worth of tokens toward a new project.

You're not climbing a ladder. You're joining a network.

The reward for participation is trust.

And the more you contribute, the more weight your voice carries.

Purpose > Product

In the crypto community, people aren't just showing up for yield.

They're showing up for:

- Open systems
- Fair access
- Decentralized power
- Creative freedom
- New models for ownership and value

They're here for the chance to shape something bigger than themselves.

A Moment That Changed Me

There was a moment — and I remember this vividly — where someone in a DAO I had just joined said:

"You don't need permission to build here. Just do it. We Build to Build. We'll support you."

That one sentence hit me harder than a record deal.

I built something small. Then something bigger. And the next thing I knew, I was helping shape strategy.

In a world where so many doors are closed by default, this space flung them open.

This Is the Revolution

Web3 isn't just "better internet."

It's community-powered capital. Cultural code. Social software.

And yes — it's messy as hell.

But it's the most alive I've ever seen the internet.

Crypto made me a participant again. Not just a user. Not just a fan. A contributor.

Chapter 9: Digital Identity and the Web3 Self

In the beginning, the internet didn't know who you were.

It didn't care.

You could be anyone — a name, a handle, a floating JPEG on a forum.

Then came platforms, profiles, and performance.

Your name became a username. Your attention became a product. Your face became content.

And your identity? It became owned by someone else.

Identity Was Outsourced

Instagram tells your story. Twitter shapes your voice. LinkedIn certifies your worth.

And all of it — every post, every comment, every connection — sits on their servers.

Controlled by their algorithms. Subject to their rules. Revocable at any time.

This isn't conspiracy. It's the contract we signed without reading it.

We don't own our online selves. We rent them.

Web3 Reverses the Flow

In Web3, you own your identity.

You mint it. You manage it. You carry it with you from one corner of the internet to the next.

Your wallet is more than access. It's expression.

And what sits inside — NFTs, badges, tokens, domain names — becomes a mirror of your journey.

ENS, NFTs & On-Chain Reputation

Take ENS — Ethereum Name Service.

Instead of 0x3874jf73ab…, you become: sam. eth

That's your web3 username. Your home base. Your signal to the world that you're in this.

You can map it to your wallet. Attach a bio. Point it at a website. Receive payments to it. Flex with it.

It's yours. Not rented from a company. Not revocable by a mod. Owned. On-chain. Forever.

Same with NFTs that represent:

- Your art

- Your community membership

- Your access pass

- Your earned credentials

In the future, your on-chain history might be your resume:

"Show me your work." "Prove you were here." "Own your story."

When Did I Become a Public Wallet?

The moment it really hit me?

I joined a new community and someone said:

“Hey, I looked at your wallet. Cool stuff you’re into.”

I was like… Wait. You looked inside my wallet?

But then I realized: That’s the new profile. That’s the on-chain you.

It’s not just what you bought. It’s what you believe in.

- The communities you joined.
- The causes you backed.
- The projects you minted early.
- The ones you didn’t sell.

Web3 identity is opt-in transparency. A trust signal. A vibe check. A receipt for the road you’ve walked.

From Stage Name to Chain Name

I used to have a stage persona. A brand. A shield.

Now, I’ve got a wallet full of strange little tokens that tell a new kind of story.

A story that says:

“This is who I was. This is what I backed. This is where I showed up.”

It’s less polished. Less performative. More real.

You Are Not Just a User Anymore

You're not just on the internet.

You are part of it.

You're no longer a data point in someone else's ad campaign. You're a node in a network of value, culture, and story.

You're not renting your name. You're owning your voice.

That's Web3 identity.

And it's just getting started.

Chapter 10: What's Next for Crypto (and for You?)

Let's zoom out for a second.

You've made it through the learning curve, the weird jargon, the anxiety of moving coins and keys and wallets.

You've heard my mistakes, my lessons, my late-night Discord discoveries and dad-level metaphors.

Now the question becomes:

What's next — for you? For crypto? For this movement?

The answer, honestly, is: It depends on what we build next.

This space isn't finished. It's barely begun.

The protocols are still forming. The best ideas are still whitepapers. The worst ideas are… well, all over the news.

But at its heart, crypto still holds a single powerful promise:

Give people control of their money, identity, and creativity — and they'll build things we've never imagined.

Crypto Isn't the Future. It's the Fight for the Future.

Right now, we're in the middle of a massive tension.

There are two paths ahead — and not everyone in crypto is on the same side.

One path leads to more centralization, more control, more surveillance — just wrapped in blockchain branding.

The other path leads to open systems, sovereign ownership, and user-first design.

Your job is to learn the difference.

Stablecoins, CBDCs & the Great Pretenders

Here's where things get real.

Governments and big banks are starting to issue their own "crypto."

Some call them CBDCs — Central Bank Digital Currencies.

Others are launching bank-backed "stablecoins".

Sounds good, right? Faster payments, fewer intermediaries, digital everything.

But here's the truth:

Just because something runs on a blockchain doesn't mean it's crypto.

CBDCs are programmable dollars.

They can be paused, reversed, taxed, frozen, surveilled — all by the issuing authority.

That's not freedom. That's control.

Stablecoins from banks? Same issue. You don't hold the keys. You don't control the supply. You don't get to audit the system. They look like crypto. But they act like the banks we are trying to evolve past.

That inspired me to build.

I wanted to capture the true sentiment of DeFi — not just decentralized in name, but in spirit. Most stablecoins still have an owner. Sometimes it's a company. Sometimes a DAO. But there's always someone holding the keys.

So I built something different: an Autonomous Stable Asset "ASA" (I "coined" the term, pun intended) with no owner, no admin keys, no backdoor access. Just pure, autonomous code. It runs 24/7. Immutable. Governed by math and executed by the blockchain itself.

No human intervention. No exceptions. Just rules, transparency, and cypherpunk-level trustlessness.

Will it catch on? Who knows.

It's just like the songs I write — some never leave the living room, and some go on to become part of people's lives.

I'm okay with creating it… and letting it go. It's open source, others may be inspired and keep "writing" the next version of it…like a song or a smart contract.

Crypto's core values — transparency, decentralization, permissionless innovation — don't live in these systems.

They live in open protocols. In code you can read. In tools anyone can use.

Don't be fooled by marketing. Follow the values.

So… What Do You Do Now?

Start where you are. Keep learning. Try things out.

- Set up a cold wallet.
- Back up your keys — for real this time.
- Contribute to a DAO.
- Mint something. Anything.
- Teach one person you love what you just learned.

That's how this spreads. That's how this gets better.

If you've read this far, you're not just curious — you're participating.

Final Thought: Crypto Is Personal Now

For me, this wasn't just about investing or building tech.

It was about reclaiming something I didn't even know I'd lost: trust in my own ability to shape my future.

Crypto gave me that back.

It gave me community. Tools. A blank page.

You don’t have to become a coder or a DeFi wizard. You just have to show up — with curiosity and intention.

If some part of this book sparked something in you, then you’re already on-chain.

You’ve made it through the noise, the jargon, and the fear. Now it’s yours.

I believe in you…

Epilogue: Your Invitation to the Future

You've reached the last page — but really, this is where the real story begins.

Crypto isn't just a technology. It's a chance. A chance to shift how power is distributed. To build systems that include — not exclude. To move from users to owners.

I won't give you a checklist. You already know what to do. What matters now is that you understand why it matters.

Crypto is more than price charts, memes, or headlines. It's about ownership. It's about freedom. It's about creating systems that are open, transparent, and fair — for everyone.

But I also want to be honest: I have concerns. Crypto gives us incredible power, but if we're not careful, it could also become the most powerful surveillance system ever built. We don't want every transaction we make — every coffee, every donation, every gift — to be visible to the entire world.

Privacy is not a luxury; it's a human right. As we build the future, we must create systems that protect our ability to transact freely and privately.

Because this isn't just about money. This is about participation. About giving regular people — not just the 1% — a stake in the world they live in.

Tokenization shouldn't just be a playground for hedge funds and billionaires.

It should let a teacher in Ohio own a piece of a skyscraper in New York. It should let an artist in Nairobi sell their work directly to a collector in Paris. It should open doors, not close them.

The future of money, art, business, and philanthropy is being written right now. You can watch from the sidelines — or you can step onto the field.

As someone who's gone from playing songs on a virtual stage to building tokens, launching DeFi projects, and starting a blockchain nonprofit, I can tell you: it's worth it.

The next chapter of this story belongs to you. And my hope is that it's a chapter where power, wealth, and opportunity are more evenly shared — where everyone, everywhere, gets to own a piece of the future.

Good Luck to you and every other human being on this beautiful planet. Go forth and prosper.

"Those who would give up essential liberty to purchase a little temporary safety, deserve neither liberty nor safety"

-Benjamin Franklin

Glossary: Your Crypto Cheat Sheet

Altcoin: Any cryptocurrency that isn't Bitcoin.

Bear Market: A period where prices are falling and fear takes over.

Blockchain: A public, digital ledger that records transactions securely and permanently.

Bridge: A tool that lets you move tokens from one blockchain to another (like a ferry that carries your coins to a new chain).

Bull Market: A period where prices are rising and optimism is high.

CBDC (Central Bank Digital Currency): A digital version of a country's currency, issued and controlled by its central bank.

Coin: Usually refers to a cryptocurrency that has its own blockchain (like Bitcoin or Ethereum).

Coinbase: A popular crypto exchange that lets you buy, sell, and store crypto easily.

Cold Wallet: A wallet that is completely offline, disconnected from the internet. Hardware wallets are one type of cold wallet. This is the safest way to store crypto for the long term.

Try This: Download a free wallet like MetaMask or Coinbase Wallet. Open it. Click around. You don't need to buy anything yet — just get familiar with what it looks and feels like. The best way to learn crypto… is to touch it.

DAO (Decentralized Autonomous Organization): A community-run group with shared funds and rules enforced by smart contracts.

DApp (Decentralized Application): An app that runs on a blockchain, not on a company's servers.

DCA (Dollar-Cost Averaging): A strategy of buying a fixed amount of crypto on a regular schedule.

DEX (Decentralized Exchange): A platform where you trade crypto directly with other people, peer-to-peer — no middleman.

DeFi (Decentralized Finance): Financial services (like trading, lending, earning interest) built on blockchains.

Ethereum: A blockchain that lets developers create smart contracts and dapps.

FOMO: "Fear of Missing Out" — the urge to buy when prices are rising.

FUD: "Fear, Uncertainty, Doubt" — negative news or sentiment that causes panic selling.

Fiat: Regular government-issued money, like dollars, euros, or yen.

Gas Fees: The cost you pay to use a blockchain (like a transaction fee).

Halving: A Bitcoin event that cuts new supply in half every four years.

Hardware Wallet: A physical device that stores your crypto keys offline.

Hot Wallet: A crypto wallet connected to the internet — convenient but slightly less secure.

Immutable: Something that can't be changed — often used to describe blockchain data or "code is law" smart contracts.

LP Token (Liquidity Provider Token): A token you receive when you provide liquidity to a decentralized exchange.

Liquidity: How easily an asset can be bought or sold without affecting its price. More liquidity = smoother trading.

Market Cap: The total value of a coin or token (price × circulating supply).

Metaverse: A shared digital world where people interact as avatars.

Multi-Sig (Multi-Signature Wallet): A special type of wallet that needs multiple people (or multiple keys) to approve a transaction before it can happen.

NFT (Non-Fungible Token): A unique digital asset that proves ownership of something (art, music, in-game items).

Private Key / Seed Phrase: Your secret password to control your crypto. Lose it, lose your coins.

Self-Custody: Holding your own crypto in a wallet you control (not on an exchange).

Slippage: The difference between the price you expect and the price you actually get when trading.

Smart Contract: Code that runs on the blockchain and executes automatically when conditions are met.

Stablecoin: A cryptocurrency designed to stay at a fixed price, usually $1.

Swap: The act of exchanging one token for another (usually done on a DEX).

Token: A digital asset that lives on a blockchain — it can represent currency, art, membership, or even real-world things like real estate.

Trading: Buying and selling tokens to try to profit from price changes.

Wallet: A tool (app, hardware device, or paper) that lets you store and manage your crypto.

www.ingramcontent.com/pod-product-compliance
Lightning Source LLC
LaVergne TN
LVHW050939210926
848482LV00013B/675
* 9 7 9 8 2 3 4 0 0 7 9 0 2 *